KNIGHT OF THE SNOWS

KNIGHT OF THE SNOWS

The Story of Wilfred Grenfell

by

R. G. MARTIN

LUTTERWORTH PRESS
GUILDFORD, SURREY

First paperback edition 1974

Third impression 1983

ISBN 0 7188 2186 6

PRINTED PHOTOLITHO IN GREAT BRITAIN
BY EBENEZER BAYLIS AND SON, LTD.
THE TRINITY PRESS, WORCESTER, AND LONDON

CONTENTS

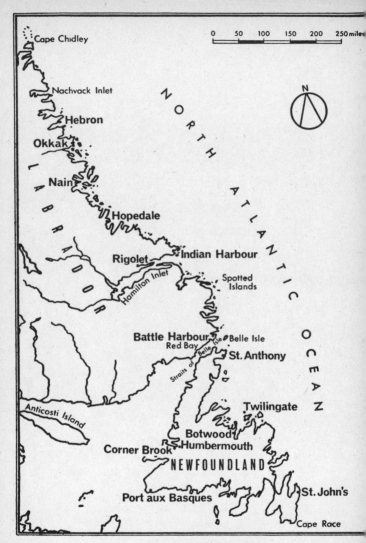

The Labrador Coast

1

"WILD WASTE GRASSES"

"WELL, Mr. Grenfell, what is that boy of yours going to be? I saw him go off yesterday morning with a gun under his arm and the day before it was a fishing rod, but I don't think I've ever seen him carrying a book."

Mr. Grenfell was on his midday walk along the sea wall when he met his friend, the doctor; and he gave a little chuckle at the idea of his son Wilfred carrying a book.

"A book?" he said. "No, I don't think you have ever seen Wilfred carrying a book. He only reads one when his mother insists that he should do a little work in the holidays."

"I saw him coming across the dunes the other day," remarked the doctor, "with a very fine brace of ducks."

"That's the only kind of thing he seems to be interested in," said the other. "He is sixteen, as you know, for you brought him into the world for us, but he never seems to think about what he's going to do when he leaves school, and he can't stay at Marlborough much longer. Why, when his mother asked him about his future the other evening, he said he thought he'd be a big game hunter!"

The doctor laughed; he had known Wilfred Grenfell from the day when he was born, and had always had a soft spot in his heart for the wild healthy boy, who seemed to enjoy nothing better than to spend his days hunting, fishing and sailing on the shores of the River Dee, where it emptied its waters into Liverpool Bay.

"I tell you what," he said, "send him round to me this evening. I'll have a talk with him and we'll see if we can get something out of him. There's plenty of good stuff in Wilfred, but he'll have to begin to work, if he's going to do anything with it."

So it was agreed, and Mr. Grenfell and his friend parted company.

The boy they had been talking about was born on 28th February 1865 at Mostyn House School, Parkgate, Chester, where his father was the Headmaster. The day of his birth had been a day of driving winds, rain and storm, as though Mother Nature knew that this boy would have to face many of her storms when he grew to manhood, and was preparing him for what was to come. He was the second of four boys, and was always a stout ally to his older brother Algernon in all the adventures they enjoyed together.

That part of England where the Grenfells lived was a land of fisherfolk and sea birds, of marsh and sand-dunes, broken up into innumerable channels which the oncoming tides were always making in the muddy banks of the estuary of the Dee. It was wonderful country for a boy like Wilfred. He never seemed to learn very much from his lessons in school, but in the evenings, on Saturdays, and during the holidays, when he was out on the marshes with his brother, or sailing among the creeks with the fishermen, he learned much of the ways of birds and fish, of the mystery of the sea and how to handle a boat.

"Wilfred!" cried his mother one evening as he ran into the kitchen covered with mud and snow. "Where have you been? What have you been doing?"

"It's all right, Mother," he replied. "I found out where some oyster-catchers were and shot them. Then I had to wade across the marsh to get them and when I was coming back with them I fell head over heels into a mud-hole. I couldn't see it because it was covered with snow. But I'm all right, Mother; there's nothing to worry about. I ran all the way home."

"Well, I'm not so sure of being all right," said his mother. "Go into the scullery and get those things off while I get a hot bath ready."

Within a few minutes, the wooden tub was before the kitchen fire with two steaming kettles of water poured into it and Mrs. Grenfell was scrubbing her eight-year-old son clean. A little later, having had a good bath and a hearty supper the young huntsman was none the worse for his adventure, but only ready for more.

The Sands of Dee provided endless opportunity for wonderful days. The flowing tides cut them into channels which changed with the constant storms, so that you never knew whether the pattern of land and water would be the same today as it was when you were fishing or shooting in it a month ago. But the changes only added spice to Wilfred's wanderings, and since none of them were very wide, and he could swim, and never seemed to be frightened, only his clothes suffered by his exploits, and as he once said, "They did not complain because they were built for the purpose."

His bedroom and that of his brother were filled with cases of stuffed birds and fish, of butterflies and moths and birds' eggs, which the pair of them had captured in their various expeditions. They were brought up to believe that the taking of animal life was only honourable when it was for some useful purpose, like food or study or self-preservation, and this was a lesson which he never forgot.

When he was not roaming the marshes in his expeditions for butterflies or wild fowl, he enjoyed nothing so much as being with the fishermen, learning to be as much at home on the water as on the land. They liked the friendly boy from the Big House who wanted to learn their craft, though experience of his recklessness taught them to keep a wary eye on him.

"Come, John, let me have a go at the tiller," he

said to one when he was out with them on one occasion in Liverpool Bay. "I can tackle this job, you know; I've watched old Dan more times than I can remember."

"Very well, Master Wilfred, but be careful; we don't want to get on to one of the banks: these channels are full of them," replied John, whose heart sometimes controlled his head and allowed the boy to do things which others would not have permitted.

At the tiller Wilfred seemed to be unaware of danger. Disregarding cross-currents and sand-banks, he set the boat straight for home, driving her across waters where no man with knowledge would dare to go. More than once they were within an ace of disaster and old John's heart was in his mouth, but nothing daunted the boy till they hove to along the quayside at Parkgate.

"That boy will be the death of me; twice I thought we were done for," he reported to one of his mates that evening.

"Why did you give him the tiller then? You might have known what he would do."

"Aye," replied John, "I suppose I should, I suppose I should." And he puffed thoughtfully at his pipe. "But he's a good lad, a good lad. I reckon he'll go far if he only lives long enough."

Neither old John nor the boy he liked so much ever imagined how far that boy would go, nor did either understand how much he was learning that was going to stand him in good stead in the days to come.

When not with the fishermen or out on the marshes on some solitary expedition with his gun, he found that his older brother Algernon usually had some exciting suggestion to make, which as often as not ended in landing one or other of them —and sometimes both—into some scrape. One holiday, as both of them were in funds, which was very unusual, Algernon proposed that they should build a boat. This was an idea entirely after Wilfred's heart and as their father approved they were allowed to spend their pocket money on materials under the guidance of a local carpenter. Their old nursery at the back of the house was converted into a workshop, and many hours were spent in the planning, the modelling, the fitting and the setting up, until at last their handiwork was ready to be inspected by their parents and received their approval.

The craft they desired was a canoe which would enable them to paddle or drift along the deep channels of the river and allow them to steal unheard upon the flocks of birds feeding at the edges. For this purpose they insisted on straight lines and a square stern. They were immensely proud of their efforts, but their pride suffered a severe fall when a cousin who was visiting them said, "It looks exactly like a coffin!" It was only too true, and Wilfred was so incensed that he immediately began a fight with his critic to make him eat his words. Their cousin never dared to make such a comment again, but the jibe remained and rankled, though Algernon maintained that, even if it did look like a coffin, that was the shape they wanted, and nothing else would suit their purpose.

Sailing and cruising among the creeks of the estuary *The Reptile*, as they named their home-made boat, gave them many a day's sport until one day, when Wilfred and a friend were using her to stalk curlew, she capsized, shot her crew into the half-frozen water, and sank to the bottom.

This was the boy whom Mr. Grenfell sent to the doctor's house that evening after their talk on the sea wall. For two hours doctor and school-master's son talked together about horses and ships, the marshes, and much else, but none of the suggestions which the doctor made as the time passed by appealed to Wilfred as a way of spending his life.

"Now before you go," said the doctor, "I'd just like you to look at this," and he reached for a large glass jar containing a weird-looking object in pure alcohol, which had been standing on one of the shelves in his sanctum.

"What on earth is it?" asked the boy, fascinated by the white puckered-up mass.

"You may well ask: it is something we cannot get on without." He tapped the boy's head with his finger. "It is the brain of a man."

"The brain of a man? Phew!" And young Grenfell held the jar up to the gaslight that he might see the wonder more clearly. All sorts of thoughts galloped through his head; this was the thing that transmitted to every part of his body all that made man, that controlled his physical strength and growth, that enabled him to think and choose and act.

For some minutes he looked at it in silence. As far back as anyone could trace all his family had been soldiers and sailors and clergymen and teachers. But, as he held the jar with the pickled brain in his hand that night in his old friend's study, he knew that *he* must be a doctor.

2

"I MUST GO DOWN TO
THE SEAS AGAIN"

IT was a great change from the marshes and creeks and wide open spaces of the estuary of the Dee for young Grenfell to come as a medical student to the London Hospital, standing amid the crowded unhealthy slums of the Whitechapel Road in the East End of London. But he was never one to grieve over what he had left behind; he was always ready to enjoy and make the best of what he had; and if he couldn't sail a boat with fishermen in Liverpool Bay, he could join the University Rowing Club and take part in exciting races on the River Lea; when he could no longer go off on expeditions with his gun to shoot wild fowl on the marshes he enjoyed all the thrills of the scrum in Rugby football when he played for Richmond, one of the crack teams in London.

The Whitechapel Road was not a very pleasant place in which to live; some of the poorest and most depraved people in England lived there in terrible squalor, but it was just the kind of place to go to if you really wanted to learn how to be a doctor, and the London Hospital, with its nine hundred beds, had some of the most famous doctors in the world on its staff as surgeons and physicians and teachers.

Grenfell soon found that he did not know much. He had learned a little mathematics and chemistry at school, but he did not know a single word about physiology or anatomy or any of the other sciences which a doctor needs to have at his finger tips. He had never enjoyed studying and had always preferred to be out in the open air. For a time after he got to the hospital he found it very difficult to learn his subjects, and because it was so difficult he almost gave up bothering until he was put into Sir Frederick Treves' class, and then his mind was stimulated and his interest was aroused.

Sir Frederick was the most renowned of all the doctors at the Hospital at that time because he always insisted on perfect order and absolute cleanliness in every part of his work.

"You must always be tidy and neat and clean, gentlemen," he used to say to his students, many of whom were very slovenly and careless in their dress, "and before you touch a patient your hands must be thoroughly scrubbed, no matter how dirty he may be. Only the best is good enough. And above all, make up your mind about your patient: no hum-ing and ha-ing. He trusts you, and you must not fail him."

These were hard lessons for some of the students to learn, but the keen ones among them knew that it is these things that go to the making of a good doctor. Once, when they were in the wards with him examining a man who had been brought in after an accident, Sir Frederick asked Grenfell what was the matter with the man.

"It might be a fracture, sir, or it might be only sprained," was his answer.

"The patient is not interested to know that it might be measles, or it might be toothache, Mr. Grenfell," said Sir Frederick. "He wants to know what is the matter with him, and it is your business to tell him. I shall come back in five minutes and I shall expect you to tell me, and this man, what is his trouble."

When the doctor returned Grenfell knew what the trouble was, and made the right answer; then his teacher was able to tell him what to do to put the trouble right. So the months of learning went by, in the lecture-rooms and laboratories, in the wards and in the Casualty Department of the Hospital. It was while he was working among the casualties that he discovered something that was doing more harm than almost anything else. One day he had to sew back a scalp which had been torn away in a drunken fight when two women had quarrelled about a sailor; here was a man whose cheeks had been cut almost to shreds by the jagged edge of a broken beer bottle; over there was a little boy terribly battered after his father, maddened by drink, had thrown him through the window into the street. Drink in those days was the curse of

England, and from what he saw of it in the White-chapel Road Grenfell determined to set his face against it.

One evening, as he was going to his lodgings after visiting an outpatient case in Shadwell, he noticed that a great tent had been put up on a piece of waste ground, and a huge notice announced that religious services were being held there conducted by a Mr. Moody. Grenfell's father was a clergyman, but he himself had never been particularly interested in religion, though he had tried to live a good life. But he was inquisitive and wanted to know what kind of religion this was that was being offered in a tent instead of in a church. So he went in and sat down; it was all rather strange and he wasn't very impressed; and when a man on the platform stood up to pray and went on praying as though he was never going to stop Grenfell decided to slip out. He was just about to do so when the leader of the meeting called out, "Come, friends, let us sing a hymn while our brother finishes his prayer."

"Ah," thought Grenfell, "that's the kind of man I like; sensible! I wonder if he will speak after the hymn."

So he stayed, and when the hymn was finished the leader, who was Mr. Moody, did speak, and was so lively and interesting in what he said about Jesus Christ and how He helps us to live a Christian life, that Grenfell decided to come again and

18

made up his mind to do so on the night when two famous cricketers, the brothers Studd, were announced as the speakers. If first-class cricketers were followers of Jesus Christ there must be more in Christianity than he had imagined. Grenfell was gripped by the way the two men spoke.

"Now," said Mr. C. T. Studd as he finished his address, "if there is anyone here in the tent tonight who intends to try to follow Jesus Christ, let him stand up and nail his colours to the mast!"

At first no one moved, and then a boy dressed as a sailor, who had come with many of his mates from one of the training ships in the Thames, stood up.

"Whew!" thought Grenfell, "what a plucky kid; he'll have a rough time from his friends when he gets back to his ship."

And then another thought came into his head. "If that boy can do it, why shouldn't I?" And he suited his action to his thought; stood upon his feet alongside the boy and swore himself in as a servant of Jesus Christ.

Having taken the plunge, he at once looked round for some Christian work to do. With a young Australian who was also a student at the Hospital he joined a group who held services on Sunday evenings in the underground lodging-houses of the district. There were some tough customers to be met there—sailors who had wasted all their money on drink, tramps who had thrown away chance after chance of making good, destitute women who had nowhere to live; he had never imagined that there could be such poverty and misery. Very often the people in the lodging-houses were glad of their visits, and several of them were helped by them, but sometimes there would be interruptions in their services, and once when his friend was speaking he had to sit on a drunken man and stuff a handkerchief in his mouth to prevent him from singing at the top of his voice:

> Pull for the shore, sailor!
> Pull for the shore!

Grenfell knew all about pulling for the shore, but he didn't think this was the time for the man to keep on shouting about it. Besides his work in the lodging-houses, he started to teach a class of boys in the Sunday School, and on week evenings he invited them to his lodgings where he taught them boxing and other manly sports. They were thrilled by the Sunday School teacher who was so good at the things they were interested in. Unfortunately, the minister did not understand boys very well.

"Mr. Grenfell," he said one Sunday, "I don't like the boys being taught boxing; it is a rough sport, and I cannot have one of my teachers encouraging it."

"But, sir," expostulated Grenfell, "it is very good for them. It makes them learn self-control and they have to keep off the drink. Besides, when they lose, they learn how to take defeat; and, when they win, they see how to treat their opponents decently."

But he was, however, adamant, and Grenfell had to give up the Sunday School class, though he did not stop helping the boys. Through sports and camps and cruises in an old fishing smack which they called *The Roysterer* up and down the Thames estuary, besides talks together in the evenings, he showed many lads how to live fine Christian lives even in so difficult a place as East London.

Then, one day, as he neared the end of his training at the Hospital, Sir Frederick Treves sent for him.

"Ah, Mr. Grenfell, come in and sit down; I want to talk to you about your future now that you will soon be leaving us," he said. "Have you ever had as your patients in the Hospital any of the men from the North Sea fishing fleets?"

"Oh yes, sir," replied Grenfell. "I'm afraid some of them are in a pretty bad way by the time they get to us. They get injured in their work, and then the only way they can get treatment is to send them with the fish in any boat that happens to be coming into port, and by the time they get here, for some of them at any rate, we can't do much."

"I'm afraid that is so," commented Sir Frederick. "I've known scores of them during the years I have been here. And some of the poor fellows have been ruined long before they get to us by the grog ships which seem to do a roaring and wicked trade out on the Dogger."

"That's true, sir; they've ruined their constitutions by all this cheap rum and whisky. It makes our job much harder, and gives them a very poor chance. The government ought to ban these ships," said Grenfell.

"The government ought, but it can't or won't. I don't know which," said Sir Frederick. "But what the government doesn't do a group of gentlemen with whom I am connected are trying to do. We have chartered a small fishing smack to go out among the fisher fleet. The idea is to hold simple religious services with the men when work permits, and to provide a kind of social centre which might be an alternative to the grog ships. We are looking for a young doctor who could help with the services and give proper medical attention to the men, and I wondered . . ."

Grenfell held his breath as he imagined what was coming. What a grand life this would be!

"And I wondered," continued Sir Frederick, "if this kind of work would appeal to you."

"It's grand, sir. I will go if you think I shall be any good."

"I do think so: will you go?"

"Yes, sir, I will."

"Splendid! I will make all the arrangements with

my colleagues and with our skipper. Our head-quarters are at Yarmouth and I should like you to go, not in summer when all the old ladies are there for a rest, but in January when the gales are blowing."

Sir Frederick stood up and shook his student's hand. "God bless you, Mr. Grenfell," he said quietly.

"Thank you, sir," replied the young doctor, and he walked out of his chief's room on air.

3

NORTH SEA DOCTOR

TO Grenfell, only anxious to get started on his work with the fishing fleet, it seemed as though the last weeks of the year 1887 would never come to an end. But at last he set off from Liverpool Street station one January afternoon to join the Mission Ship. It was a miserably cold and wet evening when he arrived at Yarmouth and a cab was waiting to take him to his ship. He could see nothing as he went along, and when at last the horse stopped he found himself on a stretch of deserted road at the back of the beyond.

"Where's the ship?" he asked the cabman.

"Well," he said, pointing to a couple of posts which seemed to be stuck in the sand, "I reckon they will be her masts, but where she is I wouldn't like to say. She can't be far away from her masts hidden by the quay, I shouldn't wonder." And the old man chuckled at the look of dismay which he saw on Grenfell's face.

Poor Grenfell! He climbed up the bank and peered down: in the darkness he could just make out the hull of a ship not much longer than the old *Roysterer* in which he had gone sailing with his club boys. He was so disappointed that he was beginning to wish he had never come when a cheery voice called out from below:

"Is that the doctor? Very glad to see you, sir. Come aboard! Come aboard!"

That made him feel better; he paid his cabby, took hold of his bag, and made his way back to the bank.

"Careful how you go, sir. Mind the rigging. It's just been tarred and greased."

But the warning came too late; Grenfell was sliding down and sticking to it, and when he arrived on the deck of the *Ensign* his suit was completely spoiled and he could have kicked himself for arriving in so un-sailor-like manner. But all his embarrassment disappeared by the warmth of the welcome he received from the skipper and the crew, with whom he quickly made friends. Quarters were very small and cramped, but everywhere was spick and span, and when in the light of the next morning he explored the little ship he was quite content with his new home.

On the steersman's wheel he read the motto of the Mission to Deep Sea Fishermen, in whose service he was now enrolled: "Jesus said, Follow me and I will make you fishers of men", while painted on the bows he saw the commands which he had come to sea to obey—

"Heal the sick": "Preach the Word"

On her foretopmast stay, just above her bowsprit

end, the *Ensign* carried six feet of blue bunting, so that all the fishing fleet might recognize her at once.

Her first voyage was to Ostend to buy quantities of duty-free supplies, which could be sold to the fishermen for less than the grog-ships (or "copers" as they were called) charged. The copers were nothing else but low-class taverns afloat, which did a roaring and thriving trade by ruining the men who came to them. Grenfell always loved a fight and it filled him with zest to know that he had some share in attacking—and, in the end, beating—those who grew rich and fat by destroying lives that could be fine and strong.

When the full fishing fleet was at sea, over twenty thousand men and boys were afloat, "the merriest, cheerfullest lot I ever met," as he wrote to his mother. He was always busy. Weather permitting, little boats brought injured and sick men to the Mission ship for him to treat. Often in a storm, men would be flung across a deck, or a boom would swing, and bones would be crushed or broken; an oilskin coat would chafe a man's neck or wrists, and salt water sores would result, as many men superstitiously believed it would only bring bad luck if they washed while they were at sea. Often gutting fish on a slippery jerking deck would result in knife cuts or hands poisoned by fish bones. More than once, when the *Ensign* rolled and tossed, Grenfell himself had to be held up by some of his crew while he performed his minor operations on the patients who came to him.

Most of his days were taken up with healing the sick, but he never forgot that he was also under orders to "Preach the Word". Whenever he could he held a service on Sundays, sometimes on the Mission ship, more often on one of the smacks, and men were ready to listen to him, not only in gratitude for his medical skill, but also because he had proved himself in all the varied work of the fleet to be a good sea-faring man. There was nothing very churchy about his services; his talks were always full of good stories, just as Jesus' talks had been: he made Jesus Christ real to them, so that they could almost imagine that as Grenfell stood among them Grenfell's Master was there too, speaking to them through him. The young doctor talked to fishermen on the North Sea just as a young Carpenter had talked, nearly two thousand years before, to fishermen on the Sea of Galilee.

Not every skipper would have him aboard his ship for a Sunday service; many of them wanted their men to work all day, and the owners of many of the ships opposed the idea that men should waste their time at a religious meeting when they could be catching fish and increasing profits. After the *Ensign* had been with the fleet for a few months the question of Sunday fishing became a very live one.

"What are you going to do, Billy, about this

Sunday business?" said Grenfell one day, when he was aboard a smack, to a skipper who had become a follower of Jesus Christ.

Billy Cunnington looked at his friend with a twinkle in his eye.

"You are coming to take a service for us. It is the Lord's day and He wants us to think about Him and to rest, so that we can work all the better next week."

"Right," said Grenfell, "I'll be here; but you know there'll be the dickens to pay when the owners hear of it."

"Well, it all depends on what they hear, and what I offer them in the way of a catch. We'll do as I say and we'll wait for what they hear."

Everybody in the fleet expected there would be trouble for Billy and for the two or three skippers who followed his example; but as it turned out the owners could not say much, for Billy's tally of fish after working for only six days was larger than that of most of the skippers who had made their crews work for seven. In time—though not without opposition and difficulty—"No Sunday Fishing" became the custom on the Dogger Bank fisheries.

But however keen Grenfell was that the fishermen should have Sunday as a day of rest and worship, he never believed in a one-day-a-week religion. When the fleet was not at sea, Yarmouth of course was his headquarters, and he noticed on several of his periods there that many of the men whom he had helped to keep clear of the drink while they were on the Dogger were dragged back to their bad old ways whenever they were in port. The reason was not difficult to find: apart from the drink-shops and the gambling dens there was nowhere else for men to go in their leisure time. Then one day he learned that an old hall in Gorleston, near Yarmouth, was for sale. Without consulting the Mission Council in London he made arrangements to buy it and at once began to go round collecting money for it.

"What's the use of driving the copers off the sea," he asked, "if we have the men at the mercy of land-sharks and whisky merchants whenever they come ashore?"

Many people saw the force of his argument and rallied round and in a matter of weeks the Club was opened with a canteen, a reading- and a games-room, a hall for worship and meetings, and a surgery for his work as a doctor. Once when he was going the rounds of the public houses with invitations to the club for fishermen, two men who had had more whisky than they could hold determined to have some fun out of him by standing in the door of the bar to prevent his exit. But they had no idea who or what he was. When he was ready to leave he took them both on for a fight and in less than two minutes they lay sprawling on the floor completely knocked out, while he was walking through the door ready for the next adventure.

And he was never at a loss for one. As the work of the Mission to Deep Sea Fishermen grew, Grenfell spent some periods each year away from the Dogger Bank working in dispensaries and social centres which had been established in various parts of the British Isles. Calls for help often came to him from people living in isolated places along the coasts or working in lighthouses or light-ships. He tells us in one of his books how one day a c ll came in from the Fastnet Lighthouse.

"We rowed out in a small boat to that lonel rock in the Atlantic. A heavy sea, however, making landing impossible, we caught hold of a buoy, anchored off from the rock, and then rowing in almost to the surf I caught a line from the high overhanging crane. A few moments later I was picked out of the tumbling tossing boat like a winkle out of a shell by a noose at the end of a line from the crane a hundred and fifty feet above. Then I was swung perpendicularly up into the air; then round, and into a trap-door in the side of the lighthouse."

When he had attended to his patient, he was once again strapped into the noose, pushed out of the lighthouse and lowered to the tumbling waves. For some minutes he dangled over the boat which was being tossed up and down, pushed this way and that by the breakers until at last his companions caught hold of his feet and pulled him into the boat.

Now it happened about that time that a member of the Mission Board, Mr. Francis Hopwood, had been sent to Canada and Newfoundland on some matters of business. When he returned he not only reported on his business to his employers, but also reported to the Mission what he had learned about Newfoundland in other ways. Mr. Hopwood spoke of the needs and opportunities of service among the fishermen of the North West Atlantic. As they listened to what he had to tell, the members of the Board knew they ought to do something about it; but who could be sent? They all knew there was only one man who could be sent; he was a hardy athlete able to stand up to hard climate, a doctor who seemed to enjoy difficulties, and a keen Christian who put his strong body and doctor's skill into the service of Jesus Christ. But that man was on the west coast of Ireland.

So it came about that one morning Grenfell received a letter which said, "Return to London at once: we want you to go to Labrador for us." He needed no second summons; he could not get to London quickly enough. Several months were spent in preparations—a ship, a captain, the crew, equipment and stores, and then in June 1892 he said good-bye to England, and six weeks later had his first sight of Labrador.

"A glorious sun shone over an ocean of sky blue," he wrote in his journal, "over a hundred towering icebergs of every fantastic shape, and flashing all the colours of the rainbow from their gleaming pinnacles as they rolled on the long and lazy swell. Birds familiar and strange left the dense shoals of rippling fish to wave us welcome as they swept in joyous circles overhead."

From the deck of the *Albert*, Grenfell looked at this land of wonder and terror. He was twenty-seven, and the next fifty years of his life were all to be given to Labrador.

4

BOUND FOR THE COAST

BUT Labrador was not always as lovely as it appeared to Grenfell on that August morning. Though it is actually not much further north than the British Isles, it has no Gulf Stream to warm it, and it is swept by the current which comes down from the Arctic regions around the North Pole, so that its coast—eleven hundred miles long on the north-eastern corner of Canada—is attacked by storms, often lost in fogs, and battered by icebergs. Its interior is little more than a vast rocky table-land, covered with forests of stunted spruce trees, and strewn with great boulders. One of the old seafaring pioneers always maintained that God made Labrador last of all; the materials that He couldn't use anywhere else He threw into this corner of the world.

Even so, Labrador had its good points: in the scrubby forests valuable fur animals abounded—fox, mink, beaver, caribou, deer—while the storm-swept coastal waters produced almost limitless numbers of cod. Despite its terrible climate and the bitter conditions of living in the country, Labrador was a land of riches, though its hard-working people never seemed to enjoy them; they all went to the merchants in Newfoundland for whom the Labradormen worked.

The people of the coast, among whom Grenfell had come to work, were of three classes. First, there were the Eskimos and Indians living in the north and in the interior, who were almost native people; then there were the Scottish and English settlers along the coast, scratching a poor living from the fishing in summer and animal-trapping in winter. They had the curious name of Liveyeres, because, as they used to say, "we live 'ere." Lastly there were the "Labradormen", who only came to the coast in the summer from the southern parts of Newfoundland for the fishing. They came with their families and for the most part lived aboard their schooners.

This was the land and these were the people Grenfell had come to serve. And he wasted no time: he had come to work and work he must. He urged the captain of the *Albert* to drive her forward, and, as the strange little ship with the blue flag of the Mission flying at her masthead drove up a narrow creek alongside Round Hill Island, fishermen's boats were quickly launched from the rocky shores and bombarded her with their questions—Where had she come from? Where was she going? What was she doing there anyway?

"I'm a doctor," replied Grenfell, "and I've come to see if anyone is ill."

"A doctor? If you be a doctor will you come and see a man who has been bad all summer?"

Grenfell did not need asking a second time; swinging himself into one of the small boats he was soon sitting in a dark, tiny, mud hut filled with smoke from the peat fire. When his eyes got used to the thick gloom he saw a man doubled up with pain on a kind of plank bed in a corner.

"Let me have a look at you," said the doctor, "how long have you been ill?"

"Three weeks or about that. I want to get home. There's no chance for a sick man up here, but there's no one going south till October when the fishing's finished."

Grenfell carefully examined the man and began to look in the medical chest he always carried with him.

"Well, I don't think we need send you home; you need some proper medicine and a little care and in a week or two you'll be as right as a trivet," he said.

He made up some medicine and pills and gave instructions to the man's wife as to what she was to do. Then, with a prayer that God would use what he had done for the man's recovery, he left a family in good heart and hope, full of gratitude that God had sent one of His servants to the coast. While on board the *Albert* that night in their worship the doctor himself thanked God for the way He had used him that first day on Labrador.

Soon the fact of the doctor's arrival was known all up and down the coast, for news travels fast in Labrador. But things did not always work out as on that first day.

Late one evening, when he thought that all the work of the day was done, Grenfell noticed lying a few yards off from the *Albert* a bunch of boards tied together with rope and daubed with tar, and on it sat a silent half-clad figure. Attracted by the apparently motionless man the doctor watched him for some minutes from the rail of the ship. Then the man looked up at him, and asked,

"Be you a real doctor?"

"That's what I try to be; what's your trouble?" he replied.

"Us hasn't got no money," said the strange figure.

"Well, we needn't worry about that to start with," said Grenfell. "What do you want me to do?"

"Us have got a very sick man ashore, if so be you'd come and see him."

The request was no sooner made than answered. A little later the doctor was guided to a tiny sod-covered hovel. A very sick man was coughing his soul out in the darkness of a lower bunk, while a poorly clad woman gave him cold water to sip out of a spoon. There was no furniture except a small stove with an iron pipe leading through a hole in the roof.

As the doctor looked at the sick man on his rough bed, he knew he could do very little for him; he had got pneumonia, a high fever and some complications. Grenfell could give him some medicine to ease his sufferings, but this man was too ill to be moved, even to the doctor's cabin on the *Albert*.

"Besides," said Grenfell to himself, "if I take him, what will happen to his family? They cannot come. Oh, if only I had a hospital and a trained nurse!"

Though he had done all that he could do for the man and his family, it was with a heavy heart that Grenfell left them.

"I called in a couple of months later," he says in his journal, "as we came south before the approach of winter. Snow was already on the ground. The man was dead and buried; there was no provision whatever for the family, who were practically destitute."

He was often horrified by what he found among the people of the coast. There were men going out to fish in unseaworthy boats, with fishing gear they had made for themselves because they could not afford to buy anything better, thus making their work much harder than it ought to have been. Women wore rough dresses made from flour-sacks, and children ran about in old torn vests with no proper covering for body or feet. No wonder, he felt, that disease and death were always taking their toll of human lives. Food, too, was always short;

most of the Liveyeres only had a few barrels of flour, some molasses, tea, cheap fat, and what fish they could afford to keep to maintain them and their families in life during the long eight months of the winter.

He only spent three months on the coast that first year, for in October, before the worst of the winter descended on Labrador, the Mission ship had to return to St. John's. But three months was long enough to make the name of Grenfell known and loved by all who did their business in the waters of the North. They were grateful for his skill, and even when that was unavailing, his courage, his cheerfulness and his care for them touched and warmed the hearts and lives of the Forgotten Folk. As from headland and creek, island and rock, they watched the *Albert* make her way south they knew he would return and he knew it too, for he had found the place where he could live his life as a follower of Jesus Christ to its utmost.

Grenfell in one season had learned to love the land of "fog, dog and cod", as he called it. As a hunter he was thrilled by the excitements of fishing and tracking; the sailor in him was stirred in navigating treacherous channels, as a doctor he found full scope for his powers, and as a Christian he was able to offer to men and women the abundant life he himself had found in Jesus Christ. This was life as he wished to live it.

But it was not only along the coast that his name

and work had become known. Back in St. John's, the capital town of Newfoundland, many had heard of what had been happening that summer on Labrador. By the time the *Albert* reached the port, most of the fishing schooners were home, and men who had been doctored by Grenfell's skill and knew what he had done for many others could not keep silent.

Many government officials and business men in St. John's had known for a long time that something should be done for their own fishermen and for the people of Labrador, and now this straight-speaking young man in a tweed suit, with his weather-beaten face, humorous talk and sparkling eyes, showed them how much was needed and what they could do to help.

"I must have a hospital and nurses and I must have a steam-launch," he said wherever he went. He wanted a ship that need not rely on the changeable and often dangerous winds of Labrador. A special meeting of interested people was called in St. John's, and while he was speaking a merchant, Mr. Baine Grieve, made an offer.

"I will give you a large house I have at Battle Harbour for your hospital," he called out.

"And we will build you two more," said an official of the Newfoundland government. "Please ask your Mission Council to send us their plans so that you may have just what you need."

A committee was formed to raise funds among

39

Newfoundlanders for all the many activities of the work. Grenfell was delighted and his hopes were high as he sailed for England to report on his first season to the Mission Council in London. Sir Frederick Treves found him a doctor and two nurses, and Grenfell himself enlisted the help of his old friend of the lodging-house days, Dr. Bobardt, the Australian.

The *Albert* was refitted for the second season, but when he made his plea for a steam-launch as well the Council said a firm "No". They felt that this young man had committed them to quite enough expense and they were not prepared to become involved in any more. But he was quite undaunted by their refusal; wherever he went he spoke of his need for the launch, till one day he received news that the needed money had been given.

He had already seen at Chester the kind of vessel he required; and as soon as ever the news came he hurried off to buy it. Given the name of *Princess May*, after the royal lady who later was to become Queen Mary, the launch was equipped for its work and taken out to St. John's by one of the steamers of the Allen Line.

When they saw the little launch the Newfoundlanders shook their heads: they could see little to admire in her. She had been built for river work in England and seemed to the seafaring folk of St John's to be nothing more than a toy boat which would be useless among the ice and storms of Labrador. But Grenfell was happy. The *Princess May* was his; he was her captain and that was enough. With an engineer, a crew of one, and Dr. Bobardt as his companion, at five o'clock on a July morning Grenfell steered his cockle-shell of a boat out of St. John's harbour for the voyage north.

5

MASTER MARINER

AS the *Princess May* chugged her passage out of St. John's northward, bound for Battle Harbour, even Dr. Grenfell wondered how she was going to behave. He had had no chance of testing her, and as she rolled along against the full force of the Atlantic Ocean he knew he must be prepared for anything. They had hardly rounded the headland when the engineer called out,

"We've sprung a leak, sir! Shall we put back?"

"Not if we can help it," replied Grenfell. "I don't believe in putting back unless we must. Try this."

He threw over a strong wooden plug. "Drive it well in and caulk it over with some of that tar in the tin," and to the engineer's surprise the makeshift repair held good against all the battering of the sea.

It was a wonderful voyage; he threaded the launch between islands and a terrific collection of submerged rocks, taking her where no seasoned sailor would have dreamed of going. His compass proved incorrect, but a little detail of that kind never unduly disturbed the intrepid captain of the

Princess May. If the fishermen friends of his boy-hood at Parkgate could have seen him they would have recognized at once the old daring, the scorn of danger, the abandon, that they had known in the boy of twenty years before amid the shifting currents of the estuary and Liverpool Bay.

He went through fog, and pushed against strong winds and heavy seas; wherever he sheltered for the night, people came to the *Princess May* for heal-ing and many a time the little ship was crowded to capacity—and more, as the doctor conducted a service and in his manly fashion pointed Live-yeres and Labradormen to the Master of the Sea who went about doing good and whom he served. How they enjoyed his talks and how glad they were to know that the One who mastered the angry waves on Galilee was still the Saviour and Friend of seafaring folk.

Caught in the gales that raged in the Straits of Belle Isle, he had to shelter in the lee of a stranded iceberg till the weather improved; then, in and out of great hulks of floating ice, any of which could have completely destroyed his little boat, he drove her hard and fast till he sighted the flagstaff on Battle Island, negotiated the narrow tickle, and made fast alongside the *Albert* in the harbour.

That night he recounted some of his adventures on the voyage to his old skipper.

"Doctor," said Captain Trezisse, "you are taking risks that no man ought to take; you'll find yourself knocking on Davy Jones' locker one of these days."

"Maybe, maybe," replied Grenfell; "but, Captain, the *Princess May* and I have work to do for God, and He will watch over us till that work is done."

But there was little time for talk or argument. The hospital which Mr. Grieve had presented to the Mission was being prepared for use. The crew of the *Albert*, the two nurses, the two doctors and many of the local folk were busy carrying in beds and equipment, arranging the wards, and Grenfell lent his hands and legs to the work. By the time the mail steamer arrived, all was in readiness; the first patient was welcomed and installed in his bed, and it was with glad hearts that the doctor and his staff that night thanked God that the first hospital on the coast had begun its work.

He did not stay long at Battle; Dr. Bobardt and Sister Carwardine were left to carry on, while he pressed on in the *Princess May* northwards to Indian Harbour where the second hospital was to be built, only to find that the work had had to be abandoned long before it was finished owing to exceptionally bad weather.

Undeterred by his disappointment, Grenfell set his course for the north, making for Hopedale. He said afterwards that it was the most wonderful journey of his life. Unfortunately, his charts were unreliable and incomplete; there was danger in every mile, but for him that only added to the enjoyment. At one place the *Princess May* got entangled with a series of reefs which swirled around her so that it was impossible to keep a course. Just when things were at their worst and Grenfell had almost given up hope of keeping her afloat, some Eskimos saw his struggles, put out in their skin boats and hauled the *Princess May* inside a narrow gut between the high rocks of an island where she could lie in safety.

Until now he had had very little to do with Eskimos, as this was the first time he had come so far north. There was much to distress him; many of them suffered from eye trouble and tuberculosis; their huts were dark, dirty and drainless; there was no fresh water supply, and garbage was piled in heaps on every vacant piece of ground. It is not surprising that for the few days he was with them he had little spare time: always there was somebody who needed his skill and his medicine. But the visit was long enough to reveal other aspects of their life: he found them to be an amazingly happy and contented people; they could not understand what he said when he gathered them together for worship, but they quickly picked up the tunes and the rhythms of the hymns, humming the melody and tapping out the time with their feet, while the gospel pictures he showed from his magic lantern filled them with joy and excitement.

One day he made some of them understand that he intended to go on up the coast another 160 miles to Okkak; difficult as it was for them, they tried to tell him some of the dangers that lay ahead and to dissuade him, but once his mind was made up nothing could deter him. As far as anybody knew, only one steam-driven vessel had ever before gone north of Hopedale; Grenfell determined to take the second, and persuaded a Dane who lived in the settlement to be his pilot.

There were no charts for that part of the coast, for nobody had ever made one, but the doctor overcame the difficulty by lashing a borrowed ladder to the launch's mast and using its top rungs as a crow's nest. Time after time he only just avoided disaster; he steered into channels often at great risk and, when he got there, found himself face to face with a vast precipice of rock permitting no way through, so that he had to turn about and find another passage.

One day, when he was cruising in these northern waters, a schooner signalling with flag at half-mast attracted his attention. He made straight for it and, coming alongside, went on board to find a young man with the globe of his eye ruptured by a gun accident, in great pain and in danger of losing the other eye as well. Quickly and deftly the doctor removed the globe and in a few days the wound had healed.

"Thank you, Doctor; I am very, very grateful,"

said the sailor, "but, Doctor, do you think my girl will still love me now I've only got one eye? Perhaps she won't want to go out with me any more."

Grenfell could see how anxious the lad was, and tried to cheer him up.

"If she is really fond of you," he said, "she'll take you with one eye as well as with two. But perhaps we can improve your appearance. You will be calling at Battle Harbour on your way south?"

"I expect we shall; we usually do. But what has that got to do with my eye?"

"In our hospital there," continued Grenfell, "we have a few glass eyes. Ask Dr. Bobardt to fix you up with one. Tell him I sent you. And if you are lucky there may be a blue one. If so, your girl won't know the difference!"

Greatly relieved and encouraged, the young sailor went off as the doctor wished him good luck.

Now September was drawing towards its end. Grenfell would have loved to stay north; he had been thrilled by all that he had seen—the massive cliffs rising hundreds of feet out of the sea, the magnificent fiords cutting into them, the long line of mountains inland lifting their peaks to the sky. Here was country to be explored and, living in it, Eskimo folk to be served and helped and brought to the knowledge of Jesus Christ. If only there

were time! How often did he think that! So much
to see, so much to do—so short a time available.
Next year he must come again. Autumn was
already laying its chilly hands on the north-
land. The sea was beginning to wear the oily
appearance which comes just before it freezes, and
he must turn south for Hopedale and St. John's.

Calling at Battle Harbour, he found that the
hospital had been full all the summer; even nearby
huts had had to be taken over as wards, and Grenfell was delighted at the work which Dr. Bobardt
and his nurses had done. He found the sailor too
one afternoon when he was on the quayside.

"Will you look at my eye, Doctor?" said the
lad whom at first he did not recognize. "I'm afraid
there's something wrong with it."

"Well, if there's anything seriously the matter I
can't do much here; you must come to the hospital."

"I don't think it's much, Doctor," was the reply,
"if you will be good enough to look."

Grenfell took hold of the sailor's shoulders and
looked straight into his eyes. "Why," he burst out,
"you're the boy who came to see me up north—
and you've got your eye, and a blue one too.
Almost a perfect match! Your lady in St. John's
will be as pleased as Punch!" And with a good
laugh they shook hands and went their separate
ways.

They met heavy weather after leaving Battle

and Grenfell arranged to meet the *Albert* with the hospital staff on board at St. Anthony, but when he arrived there was no sign of her. Though he did not know it, she had been so pounded by the gales in the Straits of Belle Isle that Captain Trezisse felt he must get her into dock at St. John's at the earliest possible moment without stopping anywhere on the way. He had only just managed to scrape through the terrible ordeals of the storms and felt certain that the *Princess May* could not possibly have weathered them.

Meanwhile Grenfell was plugging away with his gallant little launch; she pitched, she rolled, she shuddered; a great wave flung his compass from its box and washed it overboard, but the *Princess May* remained intact. Grenfell had to steer her by what land he saw and recognized from his journey north, and when he felt that neither he nor the launch could go further without a rest he hove-to at Toulinquet, only to be met by the captain of the mail-steamer carrying an order from the Governor of Newfoundland to find Grenfell and his ship.

Because the gales had been so fierce and even much sturdier vessels had been almost buffeted to pieces, news had got abroad that the *Princess May* and her captain had been lost. Hearing this on his arrival Grenfell quickly despatched a telegram to St. John's announcing that he was very much alive and proceeded to prove it by racing three steamers to the port despite leaky boiler tubes and a bent propeller, and leading them triumphantly into the harbour with flags flying and violin playing!

The little river craft that everybody had laughed at had covered three thousand miles along one of the most dangerous coasts in the world, where for the long northern stretch there were no lights and no charts. She was dented, she was damaged, but she was still seaworthy, and the doctor who was her captain was proud of being able to call himself a Master Mariner.

6

POMIUK THE ORPHAN

"I MUST come here again next year," Grenfell had said while he was on his first journey to the far north. The land and the people who lived in it drew him like a magnet and he visited both time and again. Much of the coast line and of the inland country had never been charted or mapped, and somehow, in between being a doctor and a missionary, he found time to make maps, plot the coast line, make records of currents, measure heights of mountains and gather a fine collection of sub-arctic plants.

For his later voyages he exchanged the *Princess May* for the *Sir Donald*, and later the *Strathcona* (named after the founder of the Canadian Pacific Railway, Sir Donald Smith who became Lord Strathcona), as these two ships were much more suited and better equipped for the rigours of the northern lands.

He took both ships over places where they should never have gone, bumped them over rocks and shoals that other skippers would have avoided. He usually had two or three students from the universities with him, and with these young men, the engineer, and his mate, he was supremely happy navigating his ship where no one seemed to have been before.

Weather never seemed to stop him; in fact the settlers used to make jokes about it. "Wind is blowing powerful hard," one would say, "this will bring Dr. Grenfell, you can be sure." And very often they were right: out of some of the worst weather the *Strathcona* would plough her way to some anchorage up an inlet. On some of these voyages there was nothing Grenfell liked more as a sport than a day's hunting with Bob Bartlett, the most famous of all the Arctic fox hunters.

When Bob first knew him, he thought he would test the young Englishman whom everyone was talking about, but he soon found Grenfell to be more than a match for him. Wilfred's pace was even faster than Bob's, so even he found that he needed all his energies to keep up with the doctor. When they reached their camping place one night, alongside a lake, Bob gasped when Grenfell made a great hole in the ice, plunged into the water, as he said he needed a bath, and then while he was drying himself, laughed at his companion for shirking a dip just because the water was a little chilly. Bartlett had thought himself tough, but he had to admit that he was not as tough as that!

It was when he was on one of these northern voyages, making for Cape Chidley, that he steamed the *Sir Donald* between towering mountains into the smooth sheltered water of Nachvak Inlet, where he came upon an Eskimo village and sighted the Union Jack flying over the store where the trappers brought their furs—fox, mink and caribou—to the agent of the Hudson's Bay Company. News had already gone abroad that a ship was steaming up the Inlet and by the time she was coming to alongside the jetty the whole village was assembled to greet her, and with the Eskimos, Mr. George Ford, the agent of the Company. The first hours were as usual spent in caring for the sick, having a service with plenty of hymns, which the Eskimos always enjoyed, and showing Gospel pictures with the magic lantern, which they enjoyed still more.

When at last there was no more to be done that day, Grenfell was glad to enjoy the supper which Mr. Ford provided. Long into the night they talked, for, said Ford, "I am very glad you have come: I have a strange story to tell you, Dr. Grenfell."

"I like strange stories," replied Grenfell. "What is it?"

Ford stretched his hand out to the table and picked up two letters, which he handed to his guest.

"I should like you to read the top one first," he said. "You see that it is from my Company and they want me to find the boy to whom the other letter is addressed. Read them and then I will tell you as much as I know."

Grenfell took the letters and read them.

"Who is this boy, Pomiuk, to whom this second letter is addressed?" he asked. "Tell me about him."

There was something of a mystery about both letters and Grenfell was keenly interested at once. So Mr. Ford told his story.

Pomiuk was an Eskimo boy who, as an orphan, had been adopted by a man named Kupah and his wife. When Pomiuk was about seven years old he had been taken with his foster-parents to Chicago where they were to take part in an Eskimo Village Exhibition at a Great Fair. Though he was so young Pomiuk was an expert with the whip, and his skill at flicking coins off a table and many other tricks, together with his happy nature and laughing face, proved one of the great attractions at the Fair, till one day he fell and broke his thigh, and was then only able to sit outside one of the huts and beg.

Now it so happened that one of the visitors to the Fair who had been much impressed with Pomiuk's skill with his whip was a minister, the Rev. Charles Carpenter, who befriended the boy in his misfortune. When the Fair ended and the Eskimos were about to return north Pomiuk promised to write to Mr. Carpenter. During the next few months one or two letters, written for the boy by some kindly settler, were in fact received, and then Mr. Carpenter heard no more. Try as he would he could get no news of his young friend.

"And that," continued Mr. Ford, "is where the Company became concerned in the matter. Mr. Carpenter wrote to our Head Office, and they have written to me. They know that there are always plenty of Eskimos coming here with their furs, and they thought I might hear something of the lad."

"And have you heard anything about him?" asked Grenfell.

"Not a word until the other day. Then somebody told me of a boy who is lying sick—in fact, I believe he is dying—in a tent some miles from here further up the Inlet. It might be this boy, Pomiuk. Mr. Carpenter wrote that letter to him; the Company sent it on to me and I would send it on to him, if I could be sure."

"Tomorrow," said Grenfell, "we will make sure. We'll track that tent down."

But it was easier said than done; for two whole days they searched among rocks and boulders along the shore of the Inlet.

Grenfell has himself described the search. "It seemed almost like looking for a needle in a haystack to search for a tiny tent no bigger than one of the boulders that lay in thousands at the feet of those stupendous cliffs. . . . We climbed a high promontory and searched the shores of the Inlet carefully with our glasses. There it was, sure enough, nestling near a torrent that was rushing down the cliff.

"Soon we were peeping into the little *tubik* and found Kupah's wife and a young boy of about eleven years, covered with an old reindeer skin . . . his long black hair cut in a straight frieze across his forehead, his face drawn with pain, and his large hazel eyes fixed wonderingly on us strangers."

This was Pomiuk; the broken bones had never been properly set and round the old wounds horrible sores had broken out. The doctor explained to Kupah that he must take the boy away, and got his permission to remove him to the *Sir Donald* and, when the voyage was done, to the hospital at Indian Harbour. Tenderly and carefully the boy was carried to the ship where, for the first time in his life, he was washed all over. For several days he was terribly afraid, but gradually he responded to the loving care he was receiving and began to be his cheerful self once again. Grenfell soon found out that the boy had never heard of God, and from that time on the dressings were accompanied by stories of Jesus showing the love of God to men by healing the sick and even suffering death that all men everywhere might enter into life.

When the time came for the *Sir Donald* to leave Nachvak, Mr. Ford was able to report to the Hudson's Bay Company that Pomiuk had been found and was in the care of Dr. Grenfell, who

56

was now on his way south taking the boy with him to Indian Harbour. From there Grenfell himself wrote to Mr. Carpenter, "We shall keep him until next year when, God willing, I shall take him back to the north. From your letter I think you may care to pray for a blessing on this little outcast."

Mr. Carpenter replied at once, "Please keep him in your care. Let me know what it costs. The boys and girls in our churches will provide the funds to maintain him."

And they did: for the rest of his short life Pomiuk was to know the happiness of being one of Dr. Grenfell's boys and girls.

Soon there were many of them. Very few were in so bad a state as Pomiuk had been when Grenfell found him, but there were many who needed more care and attention than could be given in the rough conditions of the coast. Families were large in Labrador; many families had twelve or fifteen children, and often when a father was drowned at sea, or frozen to death on the ice, kindly neighbours would take his wife and children into their own huts and share their scanty supplies with them. Hearts were large but larders were small, and Grenfell found scores of children who could never grow into strong men and women while they lived in overcrowded huts and never had enough to eat. He began to appeal to friends in England and America to adopt some of these boys and girls, but all the time he knew that what was really needed was a home for them on the coast. It was a great day in his life when in 1905 the first orphanage was opened at St. Anthony, where a hospital was being built. Five children made the first little family, but as the months and years went by others joined them, for Grenfell rarely came back from his cruises in the *Strathcona* without some bewildered child whom he had befriended and who now was to find security and love.

But boys and girls need schools as well as homes. The doctor had never been a very good scholar himself but he knew that nobody can live as full a life as God means him to live until he can at least read and write. And so when he was at home in England, or touring in America, he was always speaking about the boys and girls of Labrador, raising money to build orphanages and schools, persuading young men and women to come out with him to the coast and to give six months, one year, two years of their lives, to the young members of his growing family, without any reward for their work except the happiness of knowing that they were serving Jesus Christ.

And it was not only the children he thought about; when the men were away fishing and hunting there were long hours when the mothers at home had little to do. He noticed that they made mats for their houses from old sacking; he encouraged them to unravel the yarn, colour it with

58

dyes made from mosses and to weave it into attractive designs of icebergs, dogs, and sledges, which he drew for them. The finished articles were often so good that he knew that many of his friends in England and America would be glad to buy them for rugs in their own homes, so that many families up and down the coast had a little more money to buy food and clothes which they had lacked for so long.

There were, of course, some people who said it was not part of a missionary-doctor's business to start schools and sell mats, but Grenfell knew the Master whom he served. Jesus had gone about doing good in every way that opened to Him, and the doctor never forgot His words, "Inasmuch as ye have done it unto one of the least of these my brethren ye have done it unto me."

7

ICE-PAN ADVENTURE

IT was Easter Day 1908, and Dr. Grenfell was
just returning to the hospital at St. Anthony
after morning service when a boy came running
to him with a message asking him to go at once
to a log cabin sixty miles away to the south. A
few weeks before, the doctor had operated on a
young man who lived there with a disease in the
bone of his thigh; the patient had made good
progress and been sent home, but his people had
allowed the wound to close before it was properly
cleansed. As a result the thigh had become
poisoned, inflammation had set in, and Grenfell
knew that no time must be lost. He quickly had
his eight dogs harnessed to his komatik, prepared
his own equipment, and immediately after his meal
was ready to set off.

Eskimo dogs are very strong and have great
powers of endurance; when long distances are to
be undertaken and staying power is required, there
is nothing to beat them. No amount of cold seems
to affect them; Grenfell tells us that he has often
known them to climb out of the sea with their fur
covered with ice, but they do not seem to mind at
all; they use their front paws to rub the ice from

their eyes and then just carry on along the track. They have a wonderful instinct for finding their way under almost insurmountable difficulties and many times they have saved the lives of their masters.

As he waved good-bye and cracked his whip, he little knew that Easter afternoon that the dogs were going to save *his* life on that terrible journey. For the first few miles all went well; his komatik, eleven feet long with its runners of black spruce shod with spring steel, ran beautifully along the rough track until he reached a village where he had to stay for the night.

Next day, part of his journey took him round a long arm of the sea. At one point he halted his dogs to examine the ice in the bay.

"If this will take me," he said to himself, "I can save a lot of heavy travelling. Following that land-wash round the bay will be hard going. This is pretty hard; we can get to the island and then it's only four miles across to the shore. Come, Spy! Come, Watch!" and he turned the leading dogs towards the island and crossed the firm ice with ease and in safety. As he stood alongside his team on the island and looking towards the shore, the ice looked rough and had obviously been smashed a good deal by the incoming sea, but the easterly wind had packed it tightly together and it seemed safe enough.

"Yes, I think we can do it," he said to his dogs. "Away we go!" and they plunged forward eagerly until they were about half a mile from the shore when they suddenly stopped as though they sensed danger. The wind had dropped suddenly and the huge slabs of ice were beginning to drift apart: nowhere was one larger than ten feet square and around each one was only a layer of "sish" ice, small fragments broken off from the larger "ice-pans" as they pounded against one another. Grenfell knew at once that "sish" ice would bear nothing and with the whole icefield breaking up he realized that he was in grave danger and that he had not a moment to lose.

He spurred his dogs on to make a dash for it and go forward to the next pan some feet away, but they had not gone far before the komatik sank into the soft slob and the dogs and he himself were in danger of being sucked down into the icy water below the sish. Quickly he cut the traces of the harness to give the dogs freer movement; Spy, Moody and Watch pounded away until at last they stood on the flat surface of a huge snowball. With one of their traces tied round his wrists Grenfell with the other dogs was gradually hauled up and then set about getting on to an ice-pan, but this was much sooner thought about than done. Aware of their danger, the dogs did not want to move; he pushed them one after another into the sea, but always they scrambled back as though they did not understand how and where he wanted them to go.

Fortunately the doctor never moved far without his favourite black spaniel, and when all else failed to get the team to move forward he decided to throw the little dog forward to the ice-pan he was making for in the hope that the others would immediately make for him. The ruse succeeded; all the dogs were soon on the ice-pan, and by taking a running jump Grenfell at last landed himself alongside them.

"And what do we do now?" he asked himself. His komatik was gone; he could see one end of it sticking up out of the water thirty yards away; in his struggles he had lost his cap, his coat and his gloves, and he was soaked to the skin with icy water. Moreover his food store, his medical box and his flask of hot tea were all tied to the komatik and completely out of his reach.

"I must get these wet things off," he said to himself, "and wring them out," and suiting the action to the words he peeled off his shirt and vest and trousers, wrung the water out of them and put them on again singly so that the wind could blow through each garment before putting on the next. With his sheath knife he cut off the legs of his rubber boots and tied them round his body to maintain as much warmth as possible and by jumping lightly up and down he got his circulation in good working order again.

But there was nothing to eat and nothing to drink and he noticed that the current was slowly but surely carrying his ice-pan out towards the open sea, and once there, he knew it would soon be pounded to pieces and nothing would be able to save him. Even as it was with night coming on he would be frozen to death during the hours of darkness unless he could protect himself from the intense cold. There was only one thing to be done: three of his dogs must be sacrificed that he might live. So with a heavy heart he took his sheath knife and killed Spy, Moody and Watch and wrapped himself in their skins. Their dead bodies he piled one upon the other to form some protection from the biting wind as he lay down for the night with the other dogs clustered round him for warmth. He frayed some rope and mixed it with fat from one of the carcasses hoping to light it in hope that someone ashore would see the strange sight on the ice, but his matches which were in a box he always carried tied to his waist were soaked and all his efforts to strike them were in vain. He could do nothing more but say his prayers, try to snatch a little sleep and await the dawn of the next day.

All this time he had been drifting towards the open sea, but about midnight as the moon rose the wind changed, the constant crash of ice-pan against ice-pan died down and he managed to sleep till the first light of morning awoke him. And he awakened with the persistent thought hammering on his brain that he must have a flag to attract attention: perhaps someone would see it and would know that someone was in danger. He had only the frozen legs of his dead dogs for a flagstaff and it took him a long time to dismember them, tie them together with rope and fix his shirt to them. He could just raise his strange signal three or four feet above his head; the waving brought warmth to his body and he reckoned that if only his ice-pan remained large enough to stand on and was not melted by the sun or broken up by the sea he could last out for another twenty-four hours.

When, later on, after it was all over, he was describing his adventures on the ice to one of his friends, he said, "I could not help laughing at my position, standing hour after hour waving my shirt at those barren and lonely cliffs; but I can honestly say that from first to last not a single sensation of fear crossed my mind."

And it is not difficult to see why, because as his arms gradually assumed a rhythm he found himself humming to himself a favourite hymn whose words kept time with his movements:

"My God, my Father, while I stray
  Far from my home on life's rough way,
  Oh, help me from my heart to say
    Thy will be done."

He was not afraid to die for he knew that in this

world and in the next he was always in the keeping of the Master of the sea. Ever since that day in the tent in the Whitechapel Road when he had given his life to God he had tried to do His will, and if in the course of his work for God his life should end he knew he had nothing to fear.

When his arms were so tired that he must rest from his waving, he laid his matches out to dry in the sun, intending again to light his frayed ropes to give a column of smoke on the ice. But while he was busy in his preparations he chanced to look up. There! What was that? It seemed like the glitter of an oar. But of course it couldn't be! Common sense told him that even if he had been seen nobody could get a boat through all that slob ice.

His attempts to make smoke were unsuccessful and he took again to waving his flag. There it was again—the glitter of an oar!

"My imagination is running away with me," he said to himself. "If I only had my snow glasses I could be sure, but I'm afraid my eyes are playing tricks." But his eyes were not playing tricks at all; when he looked a few minutes later it was not merely the rise and fall of an oar that he saw but the black streak of a boat's hull. He had been seen, and he was being rescued; nearer and nearer drew the boat; at last it was close enough for a message to be shouted to him: "Keep where you are on the pan! We are coming. Don't get excited!"

As he had had more duckings than he wanted in the last twenty-four hours he had no intention of plunging into the icy "sish" and struggling towards his rescuers: he was quite content to wait till they came alongside, grasped him by the hand so that in their excitement they almost wrung it off, and lifted him into the boat where they gave him a drink of hot tea, wrapped him in blankets and made for the shore, with his dogs huddled together in the bows.

When they had got him ashore and had found clothes for him the leader of his rescuers told how the previous evening in the dusk his keen eyes had spotted a strange object on the ice and felt certain that a man was adrift. At once a volunteer crew was organized and all night long they had tried to launch a boat into the perilous slob ice and could not do so till morning gave them their chance. Though he had seemed to be alone through the long hours, friendly eyes had been watching and friendly hands had been preparing for his rescue and the whole village was waiting to receive him.

For a few days his feet were so frozen that he could not walk and after such an adventure, much against his will, he had to keep to his bed. Time and again through the days of his recovery, the words that had come to him on the ice kept sounding in his ears:

"Oh, help me from my heart to say,
'Thy will be done'."

When the messengers who had come for him on Easter Day returned home and found that he had not arrived they realized that some accident had befallen him. As soon as possible they got a boat and brought the young man to the hospital where Grenfell's staff attended to him so that he was soon on the road to recovery again.

A little later Grenfell had a bronze tablet fixed in the hall at St. Anthony:

To the Memory of
Three Noble Dogs
MOODY
WATCH
SPY
whose lives were given
for mine on the ice
April 21st 1908

8

RED BAY CO-OPERATIVE STORE

"I KNOW that man," said the trader, frowning at a photograph Grenfell was showing him. "What's he doing there?"

"Why, he has just sold me those furs for the cabin floor, and I took his photo while he was standing on one of them. Anything wrong with that?"

"He has no business to sell furs to you, Dr. Grenfell. He should sell his furs to me and to no one else."

"Surely he can sell his furs to anyone who will buy them, Mr. Barryton.* I paid him a fair price for them and the poor chap needed it badly enough. Surely my money is as good as yours."

"I daresay it is, Dr. Grenfell. But the point is that he should sell his furs to *me*: he knows that quite well, and I'm not going to have him making money on the side."

"I think you are being extremely unreasonable, Mr. Barryton. As I say, the poor fellow was badly in need of money for necessities for his family. I was glad to help him, and to help myself as well."

* This name is fictitious, but the incident is true.

"Maybe, maybe, Dr. Grenfell—but if you are going to pay Eskimos and Liveyeres your price for goods I am afraid you will lose the goodwill of the traders."

It all seemed very odd to Grenfell as later in the day he thought over his conversation with the trader. He had only been on the coast a season or two and had been very glad to buy from an Eskimo whom he had helped some skins to cover some of the furniture and the floor in the cabin of the *Princess May*. How pleased the man had been when the doctor took his photograph standing in the midst of his trophies as huntsman and trapper. And it really was odd that Mr. Barryton, a trader in St. John's, Newfoundland, to whom Grenfell had been showing some of his sketches and photos of life on the coast, should be so annoyed because an Eskimo happened to sell him a few furs.

The doctor thought about it a good deal in the next few months, and by keeping his eyes and his ears open on his voyages up and down he began to put two and two together. Right from his first summer in Labrador he had noticed how poor the people were; of course, sometimes there were poor catches and then they could not be paid much; but even when the hauls were good and fish were piled on the quaysides no man ever seemed to make enough to buy all he and his family needed. They could hardly ever afford to buy enough food to last all the year round; they never seemed able to buy enough proper clothes, and as for buying anything more than the barest minimum to keep body and soul together—that was quite out of the question, and they were always in debt. Every time they were paid, part of what they received had to be paid back to reduce their debt. Grenfell began to make inquiries; he found out why the fisherfolk—Labradormen, Eskimos, Liveyeres—were so poor and were always in debt. Then he felt that the system of payment that he had broken into (without knowing it) when he bought the furs from the Eskimo was not only odd; it was wrong.

What happened was that the merchants in St. John's established themselves as traders at various points along the coast of Labrador, and they controlled everything. If a man wished to make his living as a fisherman he had to be approved by a trader who advanced him his fishing-gear, salt and food, and in return claimed the whole of the man's catch. Only the trader decided what the catch was worth and none ever paid very much for it. What was worse, every trader claimed from what he paid the fisherman an instalment to cover part of what he had advanced in the first place. Payment for catches was often so small that some fishermen were always in debt to their trader; others never received money at all but only a few barrels of flour and molasses to keep them and their families alive during the winter. And the same system worked with the trappers: even the Hudson's Bay Company refused to pay in cash for valuable furs, and sometimes would not allow a man the bare necessities of life if he dared to sell a skin to an outsider.

One day a man brought a silver fox skin to Grenfell aboard the *Princess May*. Silver fox is very valuable and when he had been in England during the previous winter one of his lady supporters had asked him if he could get one for her and she would be willing to pay a good price for it.

"It's a fine skin, Jake," said the doctor, "that's worth a bit, you know."

"I know it is, Doctor. Will you buy it? We've got nothing and I must get some flour and molasses for baking."

"But don't you owe this skin to the trader? If I buy it I shall only get you into trouble and I daresay I'll have a bit of bother with him myself."

"I'm in debt, Doctor, I know. But he will only allow me eight dollars for it: that's his price for a silver fox. And I shan't have the money, for he will only knock that off my account. And, Doctor, we must have some food."

"All right, Jake," said Grenfell, "now I'll tell you what I'll do. If you promise to go at once and pay the eight dollars of your debt, I'll give you eight good pounds for the skin. It's just what a friend of mine wants. Promise?"

"I promise, Doctor: you don't know what you've done to help me and the family today."

He could hardly speak as Grenfell handed him eight golden pounds: they meant food, hope, life for him, his wife and his boys and girls.

Jake was as good as his word; he paid eight dollars off his debt and with just over six pounds in his pocket—more money than he had possessed for years—he hurried to buy the food that would keep his family during the coming months. Grenfell's share in the transaction was the look of hope and gratitude in Jake's eyes as he went ashore, a letter of thanks from his English friend a few weeks later, and a black mark in the books of the trader.

Some time later the doctor was out shooting with a friendly Liveyere who had given great help to the Mission in building one of the hospitals. They were at the gunning point shooting ducks flying south on their autumn migration. Grenfell had his gun cocked at a fine flock of eiders which were coming right over their heads when he noticed that Jim's hands were empty; his gun was lying untouched on the ground.

"What's the matter, Jim? Why aren't you shooting?" he asked.

Jim shook his head. "I've nothing to shoot with," he replied.

"What, no cartridges?"

"Not one, Doctor. You know how it is. The

fishery's been bad this summer. I got next to nothing and could not even pay my instalment back."

The doctor nodded. "I see," he said, "no instalment—no anything."

"That's right, sir. But I did manage to catch a few barrels of fish a couple of weeks ago, and sold 'em private-like, so that I could get some tinned milk and flour and a few other things we should need for the winter. But old Barryton found out and he won't let me have a cent—not even a couple of cartridges."

"Well, you'd better have a few of mine," said the doctor, "and get some of the next batch of eiders that come over."

So Jim's problems were solved for the moment, but the doctor knew that much more than casual friendliness was required if the problem of poverty was to be solved.

Things came to a head a year or two later when, after a bad season in the fishing grounds, family after family asked Grenfell if he could get them away from the coast. Men were getting desperate and Grenfell saw a chance of making real an idea that had been slowly forming in his head. It was at Red Bay on the north side of the Straits of Belle Isle that the situation was at its worst, and here he called a meeting at which he put forward the suggestion that the men should be their own merchants, putting up money for a store and hiring a schooner to take their fish to market and return with groceries, clothes and much else which they could buy from the profits on their catches.

The little house was crammed to overflowing; most people thought it was a good idea, but they shook their heads a good deal. Where was the money coming from at the start? Would it work? Who could be found as manager? What would the traders say? Everybody talked, often at once, and Grenfell sometimes wondered when they were going to stop talking. But at last they were ready to make some plans, though most of them doubted whether they would ever come to anything.

Fortunately the doctor was a man who was never discouraged, always hopeful, always believing that, if the work belonged to God, He would see it through. Though he himself was always eager to get on with any job he had in hand, he also knew how to wait.

"We must raise some money, boys," he said to them, "before we can make a start. But we can't raise money just by wishing for it. Let us stay where we are for twelve months and make the best of things. None of us have got much; let us see how much we can save by this time next year and then we will really get going."

The twelve months went by and when the men of Red Bay met they could only raise between them eighty-five dollars, and nobody can start a store with as little as that. But Grenfell had not allowed the ice to melt without doing something; he persuaded some of his friends to make loans to the new venture; he put in his own small savings; a clergyman on the coast sold a spare pair of boots to help. One poor Irishman walked many miles to see Grenfell just before the meeting was due to take place.

"It's all I have in the world, Doctor, saving a bunch of children, but if it was ten times as large you should have every cent of it for the store," he said as he slipped a five-dollar note secretly into Grenfell's pocket.

"Thanks, Paddy," answered the doctor, "that's the giving that tells."

Of course the traders had heard the talk about the proposed store and many of them were preparing to oppose and prevent it, but some recognized the evils of the old system and were ready to support the venture.

Again there was hardly standing room at the meeting and plenty of talking. One old fisherman who had been an overseas sailor put a question which everybody wanted answered.

"Doctor—I means Mr. Chairman—if this here copper store buys a bar'l of flour in St. John's for five dollars be it going to sell it to we for ten? That's what us wants to know."

Once again Grenfell explained how the scheme would work. Their own schooner would take their catches to St. John's to be sold at a fair price in open market. From the proceeds of the sale stores would be bought and the balance would come to the fisherfolk as earnings for their work. Goods sold in the store would have to cost a little more than was paid for them, for they would have to be transported to the coast. But the supplies would be more plentiful and there would be more money in people's pockets to pay for them than there had ever been under the old system.

At last they were prepared to take the plunge. William Pike, the best beloved and most trusted fisherman on the shore, volunteered to be manager and, though he could only just read and write and do sums, his pluck and his unselfishness and his reliability carried him through. Next day in high glee Grenfell chalked in large letters along the front of the building

RED BAY CO-OPERATIVE STORE

Within a year or two William Pike and the fishermen of Red Bay had made their store a great success. It was not long before all the loans had been repaid; not a barrow-load of fish left the harbour except through the store; every family was free of debt and even when the season was bad and the catches were small everybody was able to tide over the bad times.

From Red Bay the idea of a co-operative store spread to other places along the coast; in some settlements the store never seemed to succeed, but in many others its establishment meant the end of that wretchedness which had held the folk of Labrador in its grip for so long.

There was a day once when Wilfred Grenfell's Master had fed five thousand hungry folk by helping them to share with one another the little that they had, and Grenfell never forgot that God had sent him to Labrador to lead other men and women into the ways of Jesus Christ.

9

FRIENDS AND FOES

"ONE man is no man" is an old Greek proverb which Grenfell had learned at school and, though he forgot most of what he had been taught, he never forgot that. Right from his first visit to Labrador in the summer of 1892 he realized that he could never do by himself all that needed to be done; he could not be everywhere or go everywhere at once; he must have friends and helpers who could work at Battle Harbour when he was at Hopedale, at St. Anthony when he was by Hamilton Inlet. And, if the work was to be done at all, he would need to spend time in England and America telling people about it, raising money, and enlisting more helpers, while his colleagues were carrying on in Labrador.

Once when he was addressing a big meeting in London and describing how much of the sickness on the coast was due to the lack of green vegetables, he called out:

"We want someone who will grow cabbages for the love of God in Labrador!"

And before the meeting finished a young market gardener came to him and said:

"I'll come and grow cabbages for you."

"Right," said Grenfell, "good man." And signed him on.

And with the recruit's skill and scientific horticulture the hard soil and harder climate of Labrador began to produce fresh vegetables with all their health-giving vitamins.

When people are recovering from illness in hospital they are often helped if they have something to do which kindles their interest and awakens in them the desire to get well as soon as possible. Grenfell had often thought of this, but what could his patients do? Then one day while he was on a lecture tour in America he was shown round a hospital in Boston where he came upon a lady helping the patients to do simple handwork, painting, basketry. He watched her going from bed to bed; he noticed how patients seemed to have a new look about them after she had given them something to do; the ward was full of happy, industrious people, instead of listless folk who were bored at just killing time till they were discharged.

"Yes, this is the kind of thing we want at St. Anthony. Never seen anything like it before. When can you come and teach our people, Miss Luther?"

Bessie Luther laughed at the doctor's eagerness, but she shook her head.

"I can't just leave everything I am doing here and come to Labrador, can I, Doctor?" she said.

"I don't see why not," replied Grenfell. "This is just the kind of thing I'm looking for. Can't you come?"

"I'm afraid not—at any rate not just now. But if you could send two or three of your helpers to me here, I would show them what to do and how to do it and then they could teach your patients at St. Anthony, couldn't they?"

"Splendid!" said Grenfell; "it's a capital idea."

And he arranged for two women with a couple of small weaving looms to go to Boston.

But there was something about Grenfell's account of his work and the human needs he tried to meet which fired Miss Luther's imagination to such an extent that twelve months later she wrote offering her services if the doctor still wanted them. He sent a telegram in reply, "Come at once," and she came and she stayed.

Lord Strathcona of the Canadian Pacific Railway was, as we have already seen, a firm friend and keen supporter of Grenfell over many years. Thanks to his help and that of other friends, the *Sir Donald* and the two ships which bore his name were bought. *Strathcona II* was a very small converted steam-yacht, so small that compared with the other ships in the harbour at Southampton she looked more like a child's toy boat than an ocean-going vessel. But, small as she was, Grenfell was terribly proud of her and was praising all her good points as he showed a group of business men round her on a tour of inspection before she sailed for the coast.

"But you surely don't imagine, Doctor, that you'll be able to hire a man to take a little cockleshell like this across the Atlantic, do you?" asked one of the company.

"Ah, you needn't worry about that," replied Grenfell with a laugh. "I don't suppose anybody will be fool enough to do it for pay; but I don't expect any difficulty at all in getting someone to do it for nothing—just for fun."

And he didn't; as soon as he let it be known what he wanted he had more volunteers than he could do with, and the *Strathcona II* arrived triumphantly some little time later in Labrador where Grenfell himself had already arrived in order to take command.

She was a great little ship; for nearly ten years she did splendid service up and down the coast. One day a man climbed aboard her.

"Will you go ashore, Doctor, and see my old friend, Uncle Joe?"

"Who?" asked Grenfell.

"Uncle Joe Davis. You remember Joe Davis? Don't you remember coming to his house in a little open boat after you had been driven ashore by a storm? We hadn't a thing to eat. You was hungry and so was we. Don't you remember going next morning to that schooner which had been battered into the harbour and raising some food for us?"

"But that was twenty-five years ago!" said Grenfell. "I'd forgotten all about it until you mentioned it. But how does Uncle Joe manage to be alive today? Have you dug him out of his grave so that I can have the pleasure of seeing him?"

"No, no, Doctor; nothing like that. Uncle spent a few years in St. John's after that, but he had to come back because it didn't suit him. He's only ninety-four now, and if you'd come and give him something he'd like to reach his hundred."

Grenfell only needed the invitation; he gave Uncle Joe his medicine, but whether the old man scored his century or not the doctor never discovered.

It was this readiness to help whenever and wherever help was needed which drew men and women to Grenfell, eager to share in the helping. Some were paid, but they never received or expected as much as they could earn elsewhere; most of them were volunteers. Young people of all kinds gave up their holidays, and in many cases their careers, to go to Labrador where they were set to work as hospital orderlies, navvies, teachers, labourers and evangelists. Many who were in good positions—doctors, dentists, horticulturalists, experts in many fields—rallied to his call, "Come over and help us." Some of the traders in St. John's used to complain that young men and women who would not work for them for five cents a day would work for Grenfell for nothing!

But the doctor not only welcomed friends; he had also at times to encounter foes, and there was one which he had fought from his earliest days as a follower of Jesus Christ at the London Hospital. He discovered then what harm strong drink could do to the lives of men: while he was with the fishing fleets on the Dogger Bank he had had to use all his wits and powers to drive the "copers" from the North Sea; and in Labrador he continued the war.

He had only been a year or two on the coast when (he tells us) "we had trouble with a form of selfishness which I have always heartily hated—the liquor traffic. To our great chagrin we found that an important neighbour of ours near one of our hospitals was selling intoxicants to the people —girls and men. One girl found drunk on the hillside brought home to me the cost of this man's right to 'do as he liked'. We promptly declared war, and I thanked God who had made 'my hands to war, and my fingers to fight', when that is the only way to resist the Devil successfully and to hasten the Kingdom of peace."

This man and Grenfell had had several disagreements, and the doctor had been warned not to land on that sector of the coast on pain of being thrown into the sea. But Grenfell was not to be deterred by threats of that kind, and when he landed one day quite alone from a little rowing boat he found that his opponent talked big but did little. Though they had words and Grenfell was unharmed the man showed that he had no intention of curbing his practices, and the doctor knew he would have to bide his time.

He did not have to wait long. The following autumn, just as he was laying-up the *Strathcona* in St. John's harbour, he received a cable from Lloyd's, the shipping brokers in London, asking him to investigate a wreck which had been reported to them. There had been so many of these wrecks in the past two years in remote places along the coasts of Newfoundland and Labrador that the insurance companies in London had become suspicious. It looked as though some of them were being planned so that somebody could make a lot of money out of the insurance.

It was no time of the year to be sailing north, but Grenfell could never resist enterprises with the spice of adventure in them, and this was one very much after his own heart. The *Strathcona* needed overhaul, so he chartered a steam trawler, the *Magnific*, and despite the oncoming of winter storms which caused havoc to many ships that year he set out on the 800-mile journey to the north to find the remains of the wrecked vessel. They encountered violent weather all the way, and often with icicles and snow covering rigging and deck Grenfell says his ship looked like a gigantic Christmas cake. At last they steamed into Smoky Tickle, a little south of the Hamilton

Inlet, and there was the *Bessie Dodd* lying on what in summer and early autumn was a flat sandy beach, though now it was covered with ice and snow—no more than 150 feet from the very wharf where she had loaded her cargo of dried fish!

The reports reaching London and claiming the insurance money said that she had capsized, turned turtle and had lost all her cargo. But when at last Captain Blandford cut his way through the ice and got alongside her it didn't take Grenfell and the crew very long to discover that though she had been stripped of all running gear her cargo was intact, her bottom was perfectly sound and all the hatches were still tightly clewed. Except for a broken steering chain the *Bessie Dodd* was quite undamaged and it was obvious at once that the wreck was only a fake, which was what the doctor had suspected right from the start.

"Come, boys," he called to the crew, "let's get some of this fish transferred to the *Magnific*, then we can get *Bessie* afloat again and we'll tow her back to St. John's and give some scoundrel a good run for his money."

It was hard work, but they all went to it with enthusiasm; they soon had their prize seaworthy and stocked with food, water, chart and compass and manned by a small crew so that, if she broke away from the *Magnific* during the towing, she was fit to sail if not to St. John's, then to Liverpool. Slowly they made their way back with sixty fathoms of anchor chain on each of the wire cables to keep both ships together.

"Often for hours together," says Grenfell in his account of the voyage, "the vessel by day and her lights by night would disappear and our hearts would jump into our mouths for fear we might fail. But at last with all our bunting up and both ships dressed as if for a holiday, we proudly entered the Narrows of St. John's."

Inquiries were quickly started, and it was soon discovered that the owner of the vessel had entered into an arrangement with a trader to "wreck" the vessel and to claim with him the 35,000 dollars for which she was insured. Both had felt perfectly safe, for the likelihood of discovery was small. No one would think of investigating the wreck so far north during the worst months of the winter, and in the following summer she could be refitted, remodelled and renamed so that they would have the insurance money and the ship as well!

Unfortunately they had reckoned without Grenfell, who could hardly believe his ears when he was told that the trader who had planned the swindle was none other than Gerry Jewett—the trader who sold strong drink on the coast, whom he had opposed before, and who had threatened to throw him into the sea! It did not take the authorities long to discover Jewett's whereabouts; he and the owner were brought back from England, tried in the Law Courts and sent to prison.

With Jewett locked up there would be no more whisky running. And as he rubbed his hands with pleasure at a good day's work, "That," said Grenfell, "is how we 'went dry' in our section of Labrador."

10

"WHAT DO YOU MAKE OUT OF IT?"

AS Dr. Grenfell's work in Labrador grew with hospitals, nursing stations, schools and orphanages, a lumber mill, and co-operative stores dotted along the coast, the Mission to Deep Sea Fishermen who had first sent him to Newfoundland realized that it was far too large an undertaking to be managed entirely from London. So the whole enterprise in Labrador was gradually transferred to the International Grenfell Association in which the doctor's American, Canadian, and British supporters united to continue and extend the work which he had begun and maintained with such success.

Honours were showered upon him: learned societies interested in geographical discovery, medical research and social welfare invited him into membership; universities asked him to lecture; President Theodore Roosevelt of the United States welcomed him to the White House, and King Edward VII of England summoned him to Buckingham Palace to be enrolled as a Knight Companion in the Order of St. Michael and St. George. The doctor greatly appreciated all the kindness and honour he received but he always felt more at home and enjoyed himself more in simple cabins where he shared the fisherfolk's rough food and their tangy talk than when he was staying in the colleges and palaces of the learned and the great.

Once when he attended a magnificent dinner among some of the most fashionable people in Boston, a wealthy business man said to him, "And what do you get out of all this work, Dr. Grenfell?"

"Would you really like to know?" asked the doctor.

"Well I don't suppose you are in this kind of thing just for fun. You must be making a nice little sum," he remarked.

"Oh," replied Grenfell, "you'd be surprised! Have you got a few minutes to spare? I'd like to tell you about my biggest fee. I've had many of the same kind in my time; but I always reckon this is the biggest."

"Go ahead," said his companion, and Grenfell started.

"It was when I was up at Deep Water Creek, about three years ago, that I was called in to see an old Englishman who had had 'a bad place this twelve-month'. It was only a tiny cottage and there were three children on the floor playing with a young man.

" 'Are these all yours?' I asked my host.

" 'Oh, no, no, Doctor: they're his'—and he

pointed to the young man, and whispered—
'You remember Kate, his wife, who died in hospital last year.' I remembered. 'We took Sam
and the little 'uns when she lay dead. You see,
he couldn't look after them on his own so me
and mother said, "Come to us." '

"By this time I had finished the cup of hot tea
which the fisherman's wife had provided.

" 'Well, Skipper John,' I said, 'we'd better get
out and see that old Englishman.'

" 'He's not out, Doctor, he's upstairs in bed.
Go up the ladder and you'll find them both; his
poor wife never leaves him.'

"I climbed the ladder into a kind of little loft:
through the open window blew a cutting wind
and the invalid's wife, almost hidden by a thick
shawl, was trying to keep herself warm by sway-
ing backwards and forwards on a stool and singing to herself the verse of a hymn. In a corner
of the room hung a disinfectant sheet and behind
it lay the bed with an old man upon it.

" 'Uncle Solomon, it's the doctor. How are
you? No pain, Uncle Solomon, I hope.'

"A thin hand came out of the blankets and held
mine. 'No pain, Doctor, no pain, thank the good
Lord and Skipper John: he took us in when we
were starving.'

" 'He has a lot of pain, Doctor, though he
always says not. But I watch him; I know,' chimed
in the wife.

"For a long time I stood above the old man who still held my hand. Here was disease eating away the life of a good man. Uncle Solomon was past the help any doctor could give. I could only commend him to the mercy and care of God and give his wife some tablets which would ease the pain when it was at its worst.

"When I stood once again in the living-room, the children were in their bunks and Skipper John stood with their father by the fire.

" 'It was good of you to come, Doctor. The poor old creatures won't last long, I know; but I wanted you to see them. We are so grateful you comed.'

"He almost wrung my hand off as he grasped it in his thanks.

" 'I haven't a cent in the world to pay you, Doctor. The old couple have taken all we put by. But when I gets a skin in t'winter, I'll try to pay you for your visit.'

" 'Skipper John, are the old couple relations of yours?'

" 'Well, no, Doctor; not what you would call relations.'

" 'Do they pay you for having them?'

" 'They has nothing to pay with, Doctor.'

" 'Why did you take them, then?'

" 'They was homeless and hungry. The old man was ill and the old lady was blind.'

" 'Have they been with you long?'

" 'A twelve-month come Saturday. Thank you again, Doctor, for coming.' "

As he finished his story Grenfell looked the business man straight in the face. " 'I haven't a cent in the world to pay you, Doctor'—that is what he said to me; but I look upon the way he said 'Thank you' to me as my biggest fee."

The business man always reckoned to be paid for what he did, but for Grenfell the thanks and loyalty and friendship of his people along the coast were of far greater value than the salary he received from the Mission.

"Christ means to me the best kind of a Friend, as well as Leader," he wrote in one of his books, "who is giving me in this world ten times, nay the proverbial hundredfold, as good times as I could enjoy in any other way. . . . There is the terrible fact that if I had not heard the call of Christ in the tent that day I might possibly have been a physician in Harley Street (London), being driven about in my Rolls-Royce! I would not have lost the opportunity of going to Labrador for anything."

For fifty years he served there as doctor, teacher, man of business and missionary—all in the name of Jesus Christ. He lived for Labrador and when he died in October 1940 it was in Labrador by a granite outcrop high on a hill behind the Mission buildings at St. Anthony that they buried his ashes.

When eighteen months before his death he paid his last visit to the coast everybody seemed to know that they would never see him in the flesh again. "But he will come back," they said. And back he came for Grenfell is Labrador and Labrador is Grenfell and his spirit lives on in the hearts and lives of those today who carry on what he had so splendidly begun.